THE PACIFIC NORTHWEST POETRY SERIES

Linda Bierds / *General Editor*

THE PACIFIC NORTHWEST POETRY SERIES

LIGHT'S LADDER

POEMS BY

CHRISTOPHER HOWELL

UNIVERSITY OF WASHINGTON PRESS

SEATTLE & LONDON

Light's Ladder, the fourth volume in the
PACIFIC NORTHWEST POETRY SERIES,
is published with the generous support of
CYNTHIA LOVELACE SEARS.

FIRST EDITION
© 2004 by Christopher Howell
Printed in the United States of America
Designed by Audrey Seretha Meyer
12 11 10 09 08 07 06 05 04   5 4 3 2 1

UNIVERSITY OF WASHINGTON PRESS
P.O. Box 50096, Seattle, WA 98145
www.washington.edu/uwpress

Library of Congress Cataloging-in-Publication Data

Howell, Christopher.
Light's ladder / Christopher Howell.—1st ed.
    p.   cm.—(Pacific Northwest poetry series)
ISBN 0-295-98399-X (cloth : alk. paper)—ISBN 0-295-98400-7
(pbk.: alk. paper)
I. Title.   II. Series.
PS3558.O897L54   2004
811'.54—dc22   2004040716

The paper used in this publication is acid-free and recycled from
10 percent post-consumer and at least 50 percent pre-consumer waste.
It meets the minimum requirements of American National Standard for
Information Sciences–Permanence of Paper for Printed Library Materials,
ANSI Z39.48-1984.

For Emma Rifkah Howell
1981–2001

The temple bell stops
but the music keeps coming
out of the flowers.

— B A S H O

CONTENTS

PREFACE

IT IS SOMETIMES SUGGESTED that the true subject
of poetry, in the postmodern age, is poetry itself. In the case
of *Light's Ladder*, I don't think this is so—at least I hope it isn't.
The book is about states of being, both biographical and specu-
lative. What is it like to be alive in this time? To what extent do
memory, imagination, and grief (themes of the book's three
sections) color (or dictate) this experience? The book's responses
to these questions are largely arhetorical, anti-Aristotelian, are
instead mated to the tone and texture of the language so that
the poem's ideas (please God) work as drama works: by means
of a kind of immersion. My hope is that in the year 2350 some-
one opening this book will find here a familiar and authentic
voice speaking of things that still matter.

CHRISTOPHER HOWELL, 2004

I

Now in the falling of the unfailing year
The quiet clicking leaves unlatch a door
To those long landscapes we have waited for.

— ROBERT FRANCIS

If He Remembers June Light in Oslo

There was broken glass,
of course, and people were dying
as they do every minute. But, he thought,
Heaven must be this long arriving
and eternal day. So he had a beer
at an outdoor joint on Karl Johan Gaten
and thought of Hamsun starving
and of pale, dark-eyed women
who said, in that beautiful tongue, "yes,
come in." who were, even then, saying it
from opening doorways all over town.
In the palace garden

six couples were dancing under the viola
sweetness of the king's lilac trees.
Something swayed in him

as he walked near and heard the music
of their clothes dismantling restraint,
their voices becoming doves and melodies
of the body. Years from there he would remember
the freedom of his loneliness then, strangerhood
wearing him like shoes that said Listen,
there will be many likenesses
of you and many many nights, but this daylight
shall be the soul's only fragrance.
And if he remembers now
he is in love, which is the soul's condition, and alone
because that is how we live.

Running

Orange-yellow almost kite-sized leaves whispered their
descent, everything falling or hanging on through the taste
of woodsmoke and the damp vacant lots shiny with bent-down weeds.
I was there because my daily ten-mile path passed that way
under the immense gray forehead of October sky.

That was all. So when the dog came on
like a golden javelin clearing the wire fence,
I mistook him for a messenger of joy
and slowed to greet him
as Jacob must have turned from his quest to greet the angel
among thornbrakes and crying desert lightness.

But when the blur of him came, coiling for the flight
up to my throat,
I scooped the nearest stone and drilled it with the skill
terror lends
so that he fell from midair like Pegasus shot through the heart.

Screeching and foaming with adrenaline and fear, I trampled
the body and kicked it into roadside grass and gravel.
When I saw, standing by the gate, the little girl, her soundless
swollen grief, fishhooks twisting in the way
she stood, it was too late. Buttered with blood and fur, I cursed her
and ran off along the Spanaway Loop.

Each year at this time
the child, thirty-five now at least, wakes me
with her reddened watery voice.
And each year I sever my legs or carve
out my heart that she shall not have seen that day
the dancing bestial fact of skull,
fur, wings, everything
done to ruby dust.

He was just protecting me, she says
in a little ghost voice, and you come along and send him
straight back to heaven
like a bird.

There was no pleasure in it, none, I plead (lying,
like so many others, about the wanton peace that comes
with killing), it was fear he might have torn me like a doll,
sawdust trickling out onto the sodden road, all my hope just pennies
thrown away.
She lifts her arms then
and shows the signatures of blades, tongs, fists, and common
sorrow, badges
of her ravishments. And, placing my fingers in the scars, she
does a little crow-like step and sings

O happy life that's like the sun,
Come out come out, the burning's done.

Then I beg her flay me like a fish, down to the gleaming
soul, but she's gone and taken a spider's face, the many eyes
tearless, weaving an unremembrance that will not catch or hold
even the smallest essence of the years through which I fall
and go on running.

5

Metamorphosis

The moth is insane, beating
himself. Soon he will be dead;
soon he will be a dusty wreck
of paper stars wondering who
its mother is.
When light goes out, still
softly something batters the glass.
Insane. All night
I hear the rhythm of the moth becoming
lost, becoming the soft thud of sea

and the voice of a girl who loved me once
by a dark shed
and her darkness becoming mine.

Transformation happens
like this: you are so tired,
clasping the light, kissing the absence
of light, suddenly you are not yourself
and the moth passes into you
like a face too intimate to hide.
Then all your strength
is snowflakes or dust
and your name falls into a corner,
a little heap of thin wings.

Trusting the Beads

No matter what I longed for, it seemed the sea
was all there was, if you didn't count moon
and shark fins
in our wake, glittering with phosphorescence like narrow
intimations of defeat.
Even so, there was no news but the war
and unaccented rumors
of what women left ashore might choose to do.

George's wife rode off
on a Harley
and never sent even the poisoned "Dear George" we just knew
was coming for us all.
                     But blossom
begets blossom, I believed, and any breeze could be
a messenger of hope.
About my wife, therefore, I ventured to suppose
So what
if she furgles till her teeth dissolve?
So what if I die
and my body, "committed to the deep," never knows again
the silken suffrage of her skin?

Cloud shadow mingled with the bright
and salt.
The soaring albatross held to its course like Saint Brendan
trusting his beads

as a kind of chart by which intention grew into the actual
New World, forever arrived at and then
destroyed.

    And sometimes, I confess, I ground my teeth
and spat, God help her
when they let me off this tub.
       And then I thought, again,
So what?
We're all sailing off the edge like towers on a conveyor
to the blue
glow of snuffed out candle smoke.
Have any of us loved enough
if love is all we have?
      Sometimes
when the wind was up and the ship lifting and plunging
like the men
who were surely sleeping with our wives,
I stood rocking
on the fantail, tearing official documents into flowers:
pay voucher roses,
requisition pinks,
leave request lilies
fluttered over the rail and sank like votes.
Once I tossed
a typewriter and got twelve days in the brig.

At Mast, "What's the matter with you, son?" the XO asked.
"What's wrong
with the whole goddam bunch of you?"
Smartassed,
I told him it had to do with style, but it didn't.

On and on we steamed, Sisyphian, the marriages going down sordidly
in flame, grief's aftermath
shrouding the ship like haze above a village
smoldering in rain.
What was wrong would have scared the fish-like stars and turned
        our decks to soot
had it unmasked itself. What was wrong was a Hitler mannequin's
design, all of us
in rows but drifting, saluting a scrap of cloth, red-white-and-blue
        wreckage
behind us everywhere,
and the old New World a navigational distortion found by faith alone,
as Luther said
about salvation. But we were faithless, as our wives
must have known,
and dull, almost mean, with the shame of that.

Unexpectation

All right, horses come at you
in a kind of braille;
what did you expect?
They always ask you that
before the blindfold goes on
and the young lieutenant
clears his throat
and in the distance you can hear
a goat bell
and someone singing to God.
Open any door, slip your hand
down along the slope and valley
of her hips
and the brightness of total dark
surrenders itself to someone
else, or your long-dead uncle
enters the room dancing
in a checked suit.
Open the door, what does anyone
expect? The floor drops away
from all logic. Fruit trees fall
and the fruit remains
suspended, like tears, in thin air.

Imagine you've lost her and you
don't think you can bear it.
You brace yourself, but suddenly
you're a tower of shadow

without pain and all her black rose
comes to nothing, or comes
with a shout wrapped tightly to
another man's sun-dappled back
in a thicket where, it turns out,
there are *horses* the exact shape and color
of expectation's monstrous lack
of substance. The grief you waited for
becomes another
kind of grief, clouds
shredding and going back
on their multiform implications.
What was it you thought
to know? For whom
were you waiting, piquant and
blue as a diamond
dreamed up by the cutter's hammer
tapping in your sleep?
Some questions loll
with the juice of limes, pleasures
blinding your mouth.

I keep saying "you" and "your"
but what did you expect?
Confidences?
Jorge came home early
and the lime aroma of her room
made him hard.
But she was gone, a moon rolled away
from a glove.

History

At Agincourt King Henry said, "First
bastard who runs gets his jewels
on a plate," or words to that effect.
His sidekick the Duke of Gloucester
remarked some movement of the birds
in a spinney of winter birches off
to the left. Several men farted
into the pre-combat silence. Archers
on the flanks were cracking wise about
the Queen's fey scribe sent along to write
the whole thing up. There was more
farting because some of the horses
had died and the men had eaten them
to the very great distressing of their bowels.

All night it had rained as the archers
drove a bristling breastwork of sharpened
stakes that fuzzily chivalric Frenchmen
would later try to charge through
on their blindered and caparisoned war steeds.
The horse meat was raw and muddy;
though some of it, men swore, was served
by fluffy angels in blue hats. In the soup
of rain and dung and ploughed ground, those
who could sleep had thrown down in full
armor against inclines of the cold ditches.
Some whores from the village came round
but the priests ran them off—both facts

left out of the scribe's sensible and fervid
battle piece scrawled on bleached mule hide
and holed up, now, in a vault in the British
Museum.

Anyway, it was the moment before
the first French charge, after the giggling
archers had drawn back their ashwood bows
and rained a six-thousand-shaft volley onto
the noble armored heads of the Gallic cavalry,
deafening hail of ball bearings on a tin roof.
Things were quiet as could be then
for everyone, after the ringing stopped,
when up out of nowhere flew a clutch of white
doves, which circled three times between
the two poised belligerents in array and,
in the scribe's telling, "a-cryed out as one
voyse fore to taken eych mann merci on hys
enymys. And thyr was much astonyshment
befor the charage."

Later, after the wildly retreating French
horse had collided with their own infantry
tottering headlong the other way, after the English
archers had laid down their bows
and with giant mallets set to the beturtled
knights in all their shit-stained iron, someone
remarked the birds again
turned mute, crow-like and aimless as playbills
fluttering from the darkened galleries
of the next six hundred years.

Today

There is no one but a man attached to a bandolier
of dynamite. Asleep on the hard bus station bench

he dreams of children flying apart in a sunburst
he will become in the name of God and a vengeance

too necessary for careful aim or trivial concessions
to innocence, and the like. In another dream

women sort unmatchable eyes, cheekbones, and fingers.
Dust is everywhere and it is impossible to tell

if the women are laughing or wailing or merely moving
their mouths silently because silence is all they have,

though it is unlike our silence. The man keeps ticking.
What will he dream next? Abraham and Isaac? A knife

cast clattering among the stony briars? Too late for that,
the white bird on his shoulders thinks, laying a shard

of black beach glass behind the man's ear so darkness
will know him when it blooms and becomes the world.

Situation 2003

The jeweler's heart is about to freeze
or maybe frieze
and the day rises and elopes
like a bad economy
of choosing the wrong stones during a blackout.
Does this make sense? we ask. Is it
properly cut and beveled
and, incidently, what use a clasp
now that war is the President's necklace, particularly
commissioned, perfectly measured and cystalized dram
of arsenic and secret wire?
Chop chop, old man! We're going to need
to wear the sparkle of need itself,
for the cameras, you understand, and for the blowfly
god who hovers like an empty boot above the floor
of the sea, see?
And the brand new angels, waiting
for their faces and their wings,
dream of rings, the narrow
evening streets of the Heaven of zeroes
where the diamond-studded living
clean their guns.

A Party on the Way to Rome

In rouge of the night lanterns
I saw four of them rise, one trailing
a blanket, and steal to a bunk near
where I pretended sleep.
Beyond bulkheads and decks the sea
was a rushing dirge by which they cast
that blanket over the man there and began
to hit, hissing, "How's this you fucking
faggot shit!"

Most of us little more than boys, taken off
to war in the usual way, lay listening
to the curses and the cries.

When they were done, Chuck, the leader, saw me
watching and could not clear his face of angry, shamed
confusion, a man caught between what was
and what was wrong. Meanwhile
the beaten one began to scream, "You let them
do it, you just let them!" Then he went weeping
and bleeding up the ladder, the compartment behind him
quiet as a burned out church.

When the MAA, taking his time, came among us,
his flashlight could not wake a single witness
so he left, shrugging, promising Justice.

Aeneas endured the distant smoke he knew was Dido
burning. *Poor wench.* But nothing could sway him
from the path appointed. That is, the free
right life, even the very fruits of empire, was not
so far or difficult to reach, we knew, if one held
steady, unnoticed and on course, if one obeyed
necessity's goddess and could pay
with the kind of fear that pleased her. So smoke
drifted
beyond horizon's palpable secret and nothing more

came of it. So on our very own ship a man
had dared not to sail from whatever called him
master of the undivided self.
So he had loved men,
it was more than you could say
for the rest of us.

Apacatastasis

On the corner of 4th and Pike,
the man in green silk suit swings
into his litany again.
"The air is moving as if alive,
the air is moving as if alive,"
he sings, swaying slightly, his weeping
eyes fixed so that our legs pass through
the narrow shafts connecting him
to whatever world he sees.
"The air is *moving*
as if alive," he changes cadence,
pleading that we turn from our inconstancy,
that this blindness to essential light
must mean an end
to the casual heaven we suppose
we're dancing in. Of course
we ignore him, jostling to pass
out of range, almost running
as the Israelites ran from Jeremiah's
hysterical announcement: "Behold
I give this city into the hands
of the Chaldeans
and into the hand of Nebuchadnezzar,
King of Babylon, and he shall take it."
He did not say the air was moving,
though it may have been. And the blare
of traffic and bright riches
whirled about him and the sun beat down
like time.

At five o'clock the man in green
boards a bus to White Center
and sits quiet among the workers
going home. When he comes to his four-
room walk-up over the sagging hardware
store, his wife helps him off
with his coat and shoes and hands him lemonade.
All text and utterance then, even the living
air, reclines in the Realms of Rest and he says,
"What a day!
so long and swift with the air's design
I've come back almost before I left
and then
come back again, which goes to prove
that God is not a bus."

And kissing him she says, "Yes, the air is moving,
as all things, back to Him. But you, my perfect
surprise, are already there."
Then they lean into their contentment,
holding hands. Outside, a yellow traffic light
blinks SLOW DOWN above the rubble
choked streets.

If the World Were Glass

We'd all be windows for the silicone
swallows to fly through or break
their necks against, like the grosbeaks
in Corvallis, years ago. I'd be addressing
the vacant, upturned faces of the dinner plates
and bonk! this lovely green and black corpse,
wire-like toes askew, on the window ledge.

If the world were glass, some of us might
be window ledges where pigeons would
leave their little glass excreta like dirty beads
and tormented solid glass jumpers agonize
briefly before stepping out
onto the shattering air, where peepers
just as agonized would edge along
for a clearer view of glass women
in their gleamingly transparent glory.

Everything would be as it is
if the world were glass. It would be
difficult to actually see others, and hard
to go home because of confused notions
of the light, and distances magnified out of
all those proportions by which we had hoped
to live. Often the voice would crack or the heart
collapse in a heap of tailings and ineffectual
repair.

Often, in so much glare and music, we
would not know where to turn
for love, or anything else
and our great heroes would be those
who simply would not break.

The Counterchime

One night with my lover
and her husband
when I did not know how it would end,
I stood by a window in the house we seemed to share
and saw Lake Union glittering with anchor lights.
I was almost back from the war.
I felt like Odysseus
looking down at the campfires and ships, Troy
smouldering behind him, Achilles,
Patroclus, Ajax dead and gone.
He was weary and at peace with rapine,
loot, and murder, believing the gods
had played out their vicious game at last,
that he could walk right down to the sea
and shove off. Any time, he said, wind
or no wind. Row it if he had to. In a far room
the radio was playing some big band
swing and each of us at our separate stations
felt the saxophone lightness that assumes
both death and Fred Astaire. Probably
Odysseus heard flutes, lyres, someone singing.
Some geese passed, way up under the starlight, calling,
exactly on course for home. That was years
and years ago. Odysseus
would be home by now, slaughtering the suitors
and reclaiming his patient spider who wove
and unwove passion in the name of love.

Tennyson would think of him later, by the shore,
kicking stones and sighs into the cobalt Aegean.
Still later, at his desk, the poet heard his hero's
breathing, got up and stirred the fire
and read over what he'd written. He knew others
near and far lay tightly bound to bliss. The gods
were fast aslumber, Odysseus dead
and in the Happy Isles, perhaps. Oh well, he thought
of the vast oceans of the yet-to-be, blew out
his candle and turned away from the window as I would
decades down the line. Things were wrong for me then.
It was a long way home and nothing migratory
about it. Spending my love
like another man's money, I could have written
The Dystopiad of Everyday Life. I could have
rowed out on the black dazzle, trusting to fate
and the strength of my bow
bent back like the counterchime of Tennyson's footfall
as he "trod the stair" in that house
where I would some day imagine him thinking
there is too much grace in language, really, even tricky
Odysseus knew. But I stayed where I was
by the shore
and woke in a scum of cordage and ashes.
If my boat was there, I missed it
and the war was over and all of us
were gone.

Confession

It was all I wanted, to see her once
more in the lime green leaf-wash
of an early moon over water,
or anywhere at all.
I took off my head and held it, hoping
a prayer would come
or the cock-faced star bird drift
into the pooled shadows of my longing
for her arched and slippery moan
(there is nothing new in this).

I willed my feet to the poor
and lay down like a dog
in desire's lonesome collision of cries
and something said "Birds,
out of the beauty and strangeness
of their suffering, invented the trees.
To suffer, merely, is to die." So
I reassembled. Around my inclinations
snow was falling. I saw again that nothing
was new,

but a blue glass piece of it kissed me
and gave me its coin-like, deathless face
to remember always and hold against the forgeries
that were sure to lie down in my arms.

He Writes to the Soul

I'm just jotting this note so you won't forget
that though life is blue behind me and stony
in the instants I pause for, I have beads and shells
enough to hold back a sidelong toppling. Anyway,
at every crossing I kneel and say "Excelsior!"
and light a little fire in a jar and drink it down,
hoping if fire's a prayer no one will answer it just yet.
But I guess that's clear. At first I thought I'd write you
about the hemp-trap roses that grow by collapsing
and bringing home whatever's trying to sniff them
at the time, about what that means. Then I thought
that's just peering at the innards of luck, and no good
comes of such haruspicy. So I guess I'll give you
news about the lake dark which is growing, too,
and just yesterday began working up into the sky
among softball and badminton of the angels.
Lucky they were already wearing headlamps
to bedazzle the fish up there! Lucky their suede rings
keep their hands afloat, otherwise who knows
how they'd copy down the braille God keeps sending
like flocks of perforated swans? Some good news is
the apple tornadoes are out of blossom now
and have become zinc, which as you know
says very little and requires practically no disaster.
That's what Mom says, anyway, and she should know.
She says she knows about you, too. She says
you are the shade of something folded and alone
on a long leash of red pearls and that God
put you there because he couldn't help it.

But I don't know, I think you're somehow related
to this lake . . . like its language maybe, or like the idea
of swimming, which I've always enjoyed. Well, that's it,
I guess. Don't fret about my safety; if the weather
doesn't suck its trigger finger while it hunts for time,
or if something huge and golden lets me have its keys,
I'll be OK. Lake or no lake, some days I feel
perfectly disguised in front of you, like intention
around an iceberg or sunlight on the skin of the rain.
And I'm happy now, happy as a jungle, happy as a wisp
of dreaming melon and I cry only on your days off.

1974

California was burnt sienna almost the whole
way up winter's rock-strewn coast
to the Redwoods
where, when the acid wore off, we slept.
All night towering voices bent
over us the language of a choir before it sings
and the memory of it after.

              In the morning
we did not know who we were, blinking
and staggering, the sun occasionally blue
or darkened with faces. Once I saw
my grandfather hoeing in a field of trees. Frost fell
like glitter out of the reaches
until we thought, "This world needs none
of the likes of us among all these titanic
flags." Something like that, a small thought
yawing out of us bird-like and perfectly
alone. Then the truck refused to start
and we slept again.
              Twenty-four
years ago.

      Sometimes life is the cold edge
of a morning moon

still silver dollar bright and almost never going down.
And sometimes in that light
                         grandfathers
straighten and look back through bare limbs
of the orchard to tell you something's been lost,
something you're lonely for.

II

Stories for Braille Calliope

*The allegory is ended, its evils absorbed into the past,
and this afternoon is as wide as an oven. It is the time
we have now, and all our wasted time sinks into the
sea and is swallowed up without a trace. The past is
dust and ashes, and this incommensurably wide way
leads to the pragmatic and kinetic future.*

— JOHN ASHBERY

Sometimes at the Braille Calliope

Sometimes, when I wake at the braille calliope,
all my fingers stranger than the moon,
I try to halt the dream that woke me, leaving,
just to ask if it knows how long I waited,
watching it sleep inside my sleep, to take hold
its hand and quit my grieving.

And sometimes it half turns and almost waves,
a quiet black bonfire in its face.
What would I give to tell it how
distances grow solid as I pluck them
step by touch, inviting the good blind ways
creatures come to when they're tired, so tired

no light will lift them up
and nothing but absence lay them down
to sleep, or to an otherworldly music that becalms?
Sometimes I ask what would I give you, there
at an edge of my voice, to be that dream
I waited for, those hands intricately like me, turning

and reaching out as you do, possibly, writing this
to someone listening in a dark like yours?

Bird Man Stranded

My whole sadness is a wall
bent slightly to seduce the larks
or wink at the neighbor girl backstroking
her indifferent curls. A passing cloud's irrelevance
proclaims no right ransom
for the spirit, so there's nothing
I can pay. And prayer's for suckers,

so I pray: "Please return my name tag with my cash,
O God. Forgive what I forgot.
And please (I won't tell the others) send more
rich fear to scrub into my face. OK?"
But who knows what overhears
the prayers of walls?
So I become a windsock, then a fork,

then a microwave transceiver
that drinks, and rides a Harley through the park
(Sometimes I have a loyal valet!).
Sometimes I lean out
over the branching creak and sway
from which I must be gone
forever, someday, and I try so hard to see

I weep
or rain
or maybe only leak
while birds and ladders wobble at the bole
of my dismay. Of course I whistle, but I wonder
what *is* a bird man, anyway? How long
before I fly? And what is flying

but a feather-light word held to me like a wing
or like a Bible the black-frocked preacher
clutches in an attic photo, pinkish
with the loneliness of lives
that wanted what the world declared insane.
If I spread my arms and leap,
I'm only asking you to know I was alive
and vivid at the leafy mists of sky,
that something of me flew. But God alone
knows why.

The Eye Becomes Birds Because of War

Carl lost an eye somewhere
in the war.
It just rolled off like a blue
and white pill or the moon
in a 19th century novel

about the evil cleric who knew
forbidden truths and caused to occur
monstrous deviations from the usual
leafy sleep of Wessex
or wherever. Carl said he didn't

miss it, didn't matter; only the mystery,
the not precisely knowing whence
the eye had gone,
bothered him at times—as the closed
cellar door off the kitchen

bothered him when he was small
and full of voices. Sometimes
he says he thinks that lost lamp
tries to show the life it sees
now, its landscapes of abandonment

and bitter sky. In this way, also,
Carl glimpses that other "Carl"
he used to know, with his barely
disguised mother complex, his dalliances
with wives and barflies cold

as February rain, his uninformed hope
of a quick redemption. All of these
the eye suggests like a whisper
from the far end of a hall. So he can't
be sure, can't ever throw himself

into a clarity of two worlds, each reduced
in width by half. He only knows
others were dying around him, once, and
the music of their deaths was louder
than the mouths of great machines.

The eye which has forsaken him keeps
seeing men, bloody in the eyeball-strewn
mud. And it sees Carl, his face a dozen
grackles bolting from a ruined house,
half of them simply flying out of sight,
away.

The Toad Prince

Stolen things; the mosslight
lovely in a certain swale of dry birch leaves,
glittering and touched densities
touching back; her thicket
where the legs departed each
from each for starless depths of pleasure.
He would get them

into a jewelry box or palm
or pocket and would say, "This
is all you are now,
sorry, I needed the space, " knowing
they knew the big lie finally out
with small ones walking and dying
in their garage sale optimism.

They would kill him, in the end,
of course, and lift ethereally
through his vacant shape reclining on a lily.
Did he mourn that shape's prissy lack of lust?
No no no. He saw the beautiful prince
would hoard all transformation (simply
refuse its charms) but would take the kisses
anyway, and keep on taking.

King's Ex

Napoleon dragged home late
from the field where men were
struggling with death
and saw moon down the dregs
of dark
and heard cocks croak
and stretch their wings upon the gates
of nearby farms.
He was tired
and when a blue green fish began
to sing beneath his window,
he simply poured himself some cognac,
put up his feet, sighed
and thought about his mother
who had told him too many stories,
including one about the singing fish
sent by God with a message
for a greedy king.

In that story the fish asked the king
how many diamonds will you take
for your beautiful eyes?
And the king replied, "Give me
diamonds enough to fill my chamber
and you shall have my eyes,
with the blessing."

Instantly the room was awash
with gems
and the fish took the king's eyes
and devoured them like olives.

Then the king was in darkness,
running his fingers among the heaps
of stones and he cried out, "How
can I know you have not brought me
only glass?" And he wept blood
from his empty sockets
and pleaded with the fish for one
glimpse of his treasure, saying, "Fish,
 I will return you half the jewels
if you give me back a single
nearly blind eye
that I may behold my wealth."

But the fish would not bargain.
Then the king wailed, "I will give you all
but a single stone if you will bring
any sight of it at all, oh fish!"
But the fish made no reply.
Oh, Napoleon remembered the poor
king, desolate and blubbering
in his horrible dark, offering gold,
horses, palaces, lands.
Finally the fish said, I will
return you your sight, my lord,
if you give all you have named

and the eyes of your children
as well. And the king
ceased his keening and was still
a long time. Napoleon could see him,
a block of thought in a doorway,

saw him shiver, heard him
say, "Fish, I will not give you my children's eyes
and plunge them into this night
to which greed has brought their father."
And the fish replied, Now at last
you are a rich man.
And the king thanked the fish
and the fish returned to God.

Napoleon finished his brandy, thought
of Russia's vastness, and considered
the blind shadow
which had quietly entered the room
behind him.

Zeno

Poor Zeno is living still, in seeming
motion or in substance, clearly
beyond the magnitude of wishing
or collapse.
His favorite writing stick is poised
solicitude asleep in a crate of plums.
Eat all you want.
The inner sky ascends and distance,
having no object, pursues its mountain
as Achilles, even now, pursues
the tortoise of his heart swung darkly
from a nail. So change is solid
and unmoving day, old Zeno says
again. Or he may never say it
or he has always said I am alive
and happy, or at most am only half
way down the lane to death.
The true paradox
is he can no longer navigate between
thought and the stories he tells
about thought. If distinctions exist
snowy blossoms of acacia
unveil and obscure them,
and since time must be substance,
the surest knowledge lies in touching
each petal while it stays.
And so he gathers them like clouds,
or probable clouds,
in the intimate askance of his arms.

The Thirteenth Interval

Mozart went down to a bakery on the Danube and bought a baker's dozen of croissants for a penny. Eating them, walking along, dreaming of the thirteenth solitude of the indivisible, an interval which, by not existing, must exist, he strode smack into a small boy intent on trapping a dove between the walkway and the lowermost support of a marble balustrade. To Mozart's horror the boy fell head first against a step and lay perfectly still as a little freshet of blood made its way over the white stone. "My God!" Wolfgang cried, lifting the boy in his arms, "I've killed him!" At which words the boy opened his eyes and inquired sleepily after the welfare of his dove. "Forget that pigeon," said Mozart, stanching the boy's wound with his sleeve. "What did you want with it anyway? Are you hungry? You were going to cook it, perhaps? Here, have a croissant."

The boy stared at this man who had knocked him over and was now carrying him along the street. "The dove's name is Armand and he possesses the soul of my father," said the boy. "So I could not eat him." Mozart, who was not easily astounded, stopped and found himself on the Ringstrasse at noon with a bleeding boy in his arms while a mounted Royal Guardsman loomed up, lifting his quirt threateningly as he ordered them gone *instanter:* it seemed the whole boulevard was being cleared to accommodate the passage of the Apostolic and paranoid King of Hungary, in town to sign "documents." So Mozart saluted and hurried off, still carrying the boy who called out, "Farewell, Armand. Meet me in Heaven!"

The day was blue and bright with bells and the music of harnesses, scabbards, and hoofs. Serving women sweeping in front

41

of the great houses scolded after Mozart, "Look, he's beaten his son near to death!" and "Shame on a gentleman who cannot restrain his hand!" Soon a small crowd began to follow, yelling out "Beast!" and names of that kind and then to hurl fruit and shoes and bits of offal from the street until Mozart at last darted through an iron gate, slamming it after him and sprinting down a passageway, his feet slipping on the dank stones as he ran, terrified—though strangely it occurred to him to wonder why the boy seemed so feather light and then to consider why it was the corridor, which had appeared a mere forty feet long at first, was taking an eternity to traverse, rather like an infinitely sustained sweetness above high C; then, as he clattered breathlessly toward the dazzled nether opening of the passage, it occurred to him that time was not a master but a speculation.

When at last he burst forth into an octagonal brick courtyard, he found his arms empty and the walls of the surround punctuated with blue doves, cooing the names of souls which inhabited them. One bird, with a fresh scar over its right eye, flew down onto Mozart's hat and whispered, "Herr Mozart, the thirteenth interval is kindness." And Wolfgang went home brimming with a joyful sadness and with music such as no one had ever heard.

Teleology of the Airhose

Coiled and full of emptiness compressed, I feel hands
let me loose upon the open wounds of tires and dust.

Nothing is composed except in loops and rings, vague
shapes that nightly enter like the night

drawing down the door of its garage as I admire
the bolts and wrenches carefully untrussed, beaten

with a crowbar brand of hope that can't exist
unless the universe is bluntly kind. But don't ask

me, I'm of the universe of tubes and I say everything
is round and hollow endlessly, the spirit

blank but cool and hissing when it comes
and comes, a small storm leaking

through a snake, making a spindle for the lost
who lean against the dark and say, where intention

takes us is the zero's lack of heart. So listen up,
all faith is air, all mourning is the soul's tin cup.

King of the Butterflies

In the last days of the reign of John II Casimir,
King of Poland, it was decreed that two million
butterflies, 100,000 for each of his years
upon the throne, should be captured and sent up
to God, an offering of the Earth's bounty in praise
of His role in the establishment of true regality.
Thousands of peasants were set to the construction
of nets and the most delicate snares so that each
lovely animal could be brought perfect and alive
to the grace of sacrifice. Blackguards and blasphemers
were released from gaol, promised royal pardons
and gold should each deliver within seven days 1,000
of the brilliant fliers to Korbecki, Chancellor
of the Realm, Keeper of Keys and Lists.

Those who brought moths by mistake were impaled
and left to die screaming outside the Palace of Justice.
Those who brought dead or damaged goods were forced
to eat them, then to wrestle the King's bull, Njok,
whose hoofs were razors and who had never been bested.

Frequently the butterflies were brought in little cages
such as one might build to house a cricket or a god
of those slim shadows wavering in out-of-the-way elbows
of a pondside path. An entire corner of the King's
garden, jammed with nectar-bearing blossom, was netted
to contain the fluttering magnificence which, as the insects

grew in number, came more and more to resemble
a single dazzling existence, moving in undulant, serpentine
iridescence below the terrace where the King would
sometimes stand rubbing his hands as he watched.

On the seventh day the counters declared their collection
still 176,314 butterflies shy of numerical fulfillment,
which fact the Chancellor tremblingly reported to His
Majesty, who forgave him this failure and awarded him
three hours to make up the shortfall
or else.

Korbecki ran from the presence and pressed
virtually everyone he met into his personal service,
sending flocks of searchers into the meads
laden with cages and nets and nectarly enticements. The last
pennies of his fortune he spent bribing the counters (a small
army of dwarves in lace gloves) to announce that a sufficiency
of butterflies had at last been obtained. They took his money
but declined. Peasant after peasant returned with single
white admirals, or with woodland graylings almost
too small to be counted.

"What is happened, dear God?" Korbecki pleaded aloud,
at which words an old chandler approaching with a large
spotted fritillary in a reed cage said, "Excellency,
you have already nearly all the butterflies in Poland.
Would you have us bring Russian butterflies? Lithuanian
butterflies? Butterflies who do not even know our language?
Of course you would not! But happily, Sire," he said

smiling, "I have captured the King of all Polish butterflies!"
Korbecki briefly considered having the man dismembered
and fed to the royal goldfish, but instead, taking a wild chance,
bent to the little cage and spoke to the fritillary, "Oh
small but mighty one, how may I find, within the meadow
of an hour, 170,000 of your most beautiful brethren?"
And in a melodious voice the King of Polish butterflies
replied, "I have heard of this foolishness and, as you see,
have myself been caught in it. If you release me, I will send
what you desire, but this sacrifice," he said with the shadow
of a laugh, "will be quite impossible and will cost you
your life."

"If you do not send them," said the suddenly weary
and no longer astonished by anything Korbecki, "my life is forfeit,
in any case." And he opened the cage saying, "Gather them, then."
And the bright creature flew off toward the forests.

Twenty minutes later a blizzard of color blew out of a cloud
and descended on the gatherers who plucked them, tenderly, every
one. And when the last painted lady was tipped into the enclosure,
huge crowds assembled to watch the sacrifice proceed
and were stunned into silence by the beauty of the swarm,
by the fragrance of the wind which two million sets of wings
brought to them. And when the King of Poland ordered Korbecki
to torch the enclosure, to send up to God the splendor of his
Kingdom's butterflies in the form of smoke, Korbecki
wept and could not be brought to do it and the King had him torn
and eaten by wild pigs. And when the next Chancellor also refused,
the King had molten lead poured into his ears and anus. When

a third still refused, the King raged and took up the torch
himself and marched to the immense cauldron of wheeling color,
and, finding even himself unable to take so much beauty
from the world, he cut the netting and the butterflies surged up
like an explosion of confetti, like all the world's flowers
flung into the arms of God. And the King perceived
that this tribute was acceptable and complete.

It was June 1, in the year 1668. The next day John II Casimir
abdicated the throne and was carried off weeping and broken
in a cage of silver roses.

The Montavilla Reveries

I

Night and the long field vividly
asway and uncontended
under the fallen apples. Age
puts in an appearance, a tarnished horn
slung on its arm. If it says, "Winter
is upon you," in a shaky Elizabethan voice,
I feign deafness
and move closer to the fire,
which has gone out.

I I

Blackberries reach out for the old garage, slouching
almost silver, covered with birds' nests
and dried walnut husks.
Inside, the tractor is slowly becoming
a piece of sculpture
or a paleontological wonder
discovered through a broken window.

I I I

After the drugstore burned, Clovis
Johanssen claimed she cured her arthritis
by standing in the ashes
and breathing deeply.

The Fire Elegies

1 / Family Values

A man sprints to his burning house
with a tin cupful of water
and casts it savagely into huge
flames rising like birds
or the resurrected souls of a choir.
And when he stands, cup dangling
from a finger, he knows that having
fed on him like this, the world will
for awhile forgive his little
life, and he will pity even the earnest
neighbors with their casseroles and cakes.
But his wife's weeping, pointing laughter, crazed
solitude of the children imagining
poached goldfish, parakeets
black and small as nails: no answering these,
he knows, and nothing to do but run
back down the hill with that tin cup
whistling against the last good breeze
of summer, and dip it
in the moonstruck creek and run
again, carefully, up hope's incline
toward the flames.

2 / The Double Suicide of Marriage

The aspen were shivering as they do
because of cold sunlight at the edge of such
vastness. And various agencies made truth
opaque, in that way in which the soft whiteness
of sleeping crows is invisible. A few
rocks fell into the distances of sound
announcing some things ended
and some corrections worked loose
of the plainest, most honest face.

Discarding all stories, we found it

giddy to climb alone
up the bare thigh of an incline, beyond
handholds and restraints, beyond a Jack
London–like blaze and the ukulele musings
of minds gone starkly quiet in the high
eternities of cold. It was a long
way down. We held each other's breath
and launched out cleanly into air, one word
at a time shaking like golden leaves, like fire.

3 / To Build a Fire

I build it like a dwelling for the spirit
of a bird, and set the skirts alight
and lean down, kissing the spark until it flares
like thought of someone sweetly gone
but appearing now
through a window in the flames.

Cadet Pilot Terry undrowns there.
All four of my grandparents
hop around in their smiles
and a beloved dog flickers to life, running mad
with happiness after rabbits too slow to be true.
There the loose bomb does not blossom

just aft of the #3 elevator so that Mel Quinner
does not rain down on us like one
of the seven plagues and I am not ordered to type, "Dear
Mr. and Mrs. Quinner, words cannot express. . . ."
And there in the flames Hendrie, at his ease,
tends geraniums and cigarettes and forty dollar gin.

What am I bid for this lens on what's missing
and what hurts? Imagine you're St. Joan
embracing the screech, dancing as flesh
peels away and you translate to smoky sky,
a wheel refracted out of time. What am I bid
for the care and horror of those onlookers

who thought they knew what fire was for?
If it's only memory and can't burn you, still
we are each of us combustibly alone, so listen,
here's the deal: at the end a sudden spirit
flies from everyone to everyone, calling names,
burning bright with this knowledge that fire

is what we're made for, that all our lives we've
built this pyre of missing parts that we've become.

4 / Storm

The snow pours down from immense gray buckets,
obscuring the shadows of trees.
A mailman sails past like a gun blue blanket
scattering love letters and bills.
At the bird feeder five squirrels screech and posture
over thieving rights, and in the street lost
blind cars nose all directions, trumpeting sadly
or snarling with repressed violence. The familiar
is become an outsized wedding cake of chilled
disaster for which nothing can be done.
From windows all up and down our block, the round
bright faces of children peer out like flames.

5 / Arrivals

I enter the trees, a last mile,
wobblingly convinced
by appearances.
Nothing will arrest me now
that Mars is up and my path
tight and clear as a signal
on a thorn. I have only to go on
rending the seams of my fearful
nature. I have only to beast
when beast must be.

That's the way.

One step and then another step
before you know. All must proceed
into the flexing shadow, heaven
of lost gloves and pencil ends.
It is useless to struggle. Mute assemblages
of moss
wait for more moss, everyone.

That's the way.

Praise for rough roads in their certain
interminable consequence.
That glow in the homey window,
when we finally arrive, turns out
is the house afire.

6 / The Angels of Rescue
—for Bob Gregory

When they found the old hero
he had been dreaming cloud-battered
embankments of seals rolling and barking
with light blue robustness, dipping
and sliding against the still heavens
of scrimshaw.
            When he attempted speech,
caribou rose from his hair. When he gestured for water,
ice carvings exploded
like laughter in the tunnel of love.

Some of the sky bent down
over thoughts he had let go, the boat of them
a sinuous and fading name.
                        That's all right,
they said, blow out those candle-like sorrows, just send them
away. Things die, they said, mountains
gather and disperse like choristers, like horses
in tides of the grass. Things dream of seals and come home
empty as a perfect day. They said your bones are lighter now
and will not impede the semaphore of wings,
if that's what you want.
                        Or if you want,
become the seals or sunset
or a pod of whales. Your choice, really, they said
we're just here to explain

               where you get your ticket
and how distant and how lovely your remorse
when you begin to hear us, and the frost and struggle
of survival turn to faces of old friends
who speak so softly you'll think you never knew them
or wanted what they knew.

They said, we are the ice blue tongues of bells the seals
        embrace
as they rise up and descend the changeling salts of color,
        infinite
and hopeless and complete.
                       Come with us, they said.
And when I arrived I saw them
standing empty in a sea-bright column of cold
beside the fire.

A *Christmas Ode After the Fashion of Michael Heffernan and Dedicated to Him and His Bride*

Rilke believed in an immortal essence to which one returned
by means of transformation, such as that the poet will
sometimes ignite, flying "beyond all substance"
like a surprised and flaming angel made of strophes and little bells.
It was a child-is-father-of-the-man
sort of thing and a continuing accomplishment of sheerest faith
in the Cheshire vicissitudes of art. And I'll not deny
that in spite of deceits and mockeries I myself have lived
and given over into speech, at times
when laboring at my staves or rummaging in that room of the brain
that breeds them, I've felt the tidal surge of a sweetness reborn.
Last night, for instance, in my dream I held extensive and studied
conversation with my cat, who was strong for the undeniability
of Prime Cause as a sort of *Via Positiva* by which faith and all mortal
acts of conscience are set palpably free of mathematical oppressions.
"But how then," I wanted to know, "is Prime Cause established
as over against circularities of the Taoists, and others, who insist
primacy is eternal completion, the one hand clapping,
so to speak?" I put this civilly enough, and he acknowledging
through the milk that was clinging to his whiskers said, "Ah, but
are we not born? Is not each belighted instant the creation *restored*
so that Prime Cause is shown us and in us always, our very
longings the proof of grace—and grace proof of the ineffable hand?"

And as I was lighting my pipe to consider this
a garbage truck burst into the room and flattened him like an
        old hat
and I woke with missing him so profoundly I went out
scantily into the snow and brought him from under the porch
and set him a bowl of turkey drippings on the moon-bathed floor
and said, "Certainly you're right, Prime Cause is clear as night
        from dawn,"
which had him purring with wonder at my transformation,
        so long
in coming, so home-like and easy at the dark edge of day.

Heaven

So come home
along the dusty hickory-shaded ruts
with scotch broom ablaze
and orchards rising behind the sharp green
of berry fields. Come on ahead
if you can, with your fractures and played out
luck, your shoes that have forgotten
and had to be carried.
Come with steel-colored hair and slivers
of music half embedded in your heavy arms.
Did you think they would know you
topping the rise, smiling in so much
quiet it must be Sunday here
but it isn't? Did you suppose Jesus
here, too, suffering the little children,
preaching to the hill?
Whatever you thought, come on
having got so far, having found permission
for this finally-blue-again sky, dense
with robins and their singing.
The ice man's here, and the occasional horse
before a plough
and men and women who've risen
and walked here happily all their lives
and who've had so little but this happiness
they can't imagine why you've been away.

III

. . . call me, I am here,
I am right beside you
though you cannot know.

— D. NURKSE

Why the River Is Always Laughing

The white spiders have fallen like blossoms;
or the other way around (equally true).
But whatever the pale travelers have been
they are melting like good days
into grasses where the green green turtle wakes
alone
in a certain season
and wonders whence and what is this
whiteness drifting into shadow beneath him.
If I put my face down there among the blades
smelling of death and sun
and the sexual yearning that binds them,
the light creatures that have loved me
fade from me also and descend
and become all there is to stand upon
or kiss. This is what the turtle finally sings about
and the beautiful spiders
and the grass changing to a spray of lamps
(and back) before you know.
This is the untranslatable obsidian book
that reads itself. And this is why
the river is always laughing, even when you drown,
even when you want, more than anything, to drown
and every river lets you live.

Galileo

My loneliness is a secret machine,
a flying featherbed in the blue
of a hydrangea like those we set
beside the fence in Padua.
It is the language of shells, this
condition. The priest in his little room
at midnight hears it
just under the voice of his shoe
as he places it among his world of things.
The woman lying naked by someone
she detests hears it in the roar
of his breath. So it is not really mine
alone, though it is exquisitely
of myself alone in the tide and hum
of all separations, in the doorlatch
snapping to and in wood
creaking under bodies moving off
like clouds before the wind
that never comes back. So much is vacant
glance and the counting of change.
So much is the nave collapsed
and forgetting its lines and it seems
I am like others, I don't know
which of the dead believed me when I said

I'm here with a message
(perhaps they thought I said *massage*).
Does anyone want a secret that flies
invisibly in its color,
that runs on like the mind
of a moon?

Story Time

What is this about? I ask, holding
     the book
up to my son's shining face.

Again he doesn't answer, so I say, "See
     the lonely robin
wants to talk with the worm

but the moon is like a train, too loud,
     the clouds
have all run off over the big sky."

"Oh, me," he says, "rocket bus
     magic
night / moon / stars"

"But the robin, on the next page
     he's flying. Why
won't he stay with his friends?" I ask

gently, but he's through with me now.
     His hands ascend
like windblown leaves in search

of the Milky Way of sleeker, more loyal
        birds, where
no one is autistic and no huge people

live in sadness because of the boy
        who looks at them
and calls out strangely, and cannot say

the perfect words they long to hear.

All Day at the Brainard Pioneer Cemetery

I

It is said of grief
it dwindles
with time, like a suitcase
carried slowly off down the road
by a blind man.
But what if my blind man stumbles,
sits down on the battered
blue belt-strapped bag
and lights a cigarette
with one of the black flames
which leak from his eyes and fly up
like angels?
What if he brings his face
into his hands and says it's no use,
his shoes are broken,
the sun wants him dead and the bag
is so dense with grief's amazement
I'll have to carry it myself?

I I

It is not night at all,
nor the shadow of a bird,
only my own
shadow tracing the chiseled letters,

dropping the roses and collecting them again
like pieces of a story, like shoes.
Rhinestones
shine in the cracked blue sockets
of dusk's teacup.
Nearby
King David cries, "Absalom, Absalom,"
letting all arrogance and time
go, letting history take what it wants

and get out.
Around us, in the vanished fields
and farms, ghost horses plod
into their enormous quiet
and birdsong turns to bare fingers
of the winter trees.

"I will lift up mine eyes unto the hills,"
sings the minstrel whose harp brought Saul
to tears. So I, too, lift up mine eyes, following
all the empty roads, turning out
my pockets, casting off my shoes that brim
with cold.
"From whence cometh my help?" he cries
and all the living
and the dead are listening to know.

Among rotting apples and the tilted stones,
I and this old king in the gold
of our brokenness
call out, "My child, my child,
how can this be?"

III

Trouble is

we've all come home at once
and the smoke of an absence there
is deafening our blossoms.

Did I say something grand
to an hourglass?
Did she come through the indigo hedge

of that far burning other
shore? Either way, quiet as a name
I'm handing out the cold

that keeps us walking.
Quiet as the cold star sister
in my window, done

with loneliness
I'm rocking a little tower
of leaves. Red and precious

who knows why
or how to live in these
empty rooms, but I remember

what love is
and hold on to that.

Backyard Astronomy

The crockery of Heaven clanks and wanders
in a movement so immense it seems
like stillness when we're out back
on a blanket, watching the dark dust
enter roofs and leaves and then
part vaguely for the airplanes, pinkish
and edgy and slow as the approach
of a disaster. We're a family, we're in love
with what it seems we're feeling
and we don't know what to say.
God or the color of our sensation
brings small, barn-shaped impressions
through our shoulderblades, which makes us
shiver and think of other lives
behind us, to which we might turn
smiling and confused. But we don't.
We say, "Look at that bright one
over there by the plum tree, the one
wiping its eyes."

Letter

Of bees or their sky or the tiny
linkages by which rain descends its cloudy
enlacements, knowledge is mainly virtual
and not what you'd hunger for.
And if we spoke, what *could* I, lost here
because of you, tell? Your absence
is a room of gray boards
in the house of what is necessary simply
to live. Not that I mean
to bring you down from the heights of death

just to listen to me bitch and suffer
my puny need. But I want to be clear
about how strange it is to wake in the mundane
shambles you have left us, these reforestations
of muted piccolo and lawn mower lament.
I wish I were more disappointed and less unhappy,
is what I'm trying to tell you, if you are, as I suspect,
close by. Note my steady, even voice wandering
on and on, bee-like, as if you had not
in some few summer days

left me almost speechless with the rain and whir
and spinal jazz of happiness, as if my
words now were payment for not believing you
were mortal and therefore beyond proof
or keeping.

Cole Porter

The fisherman stands as always
between dark and what may be
the shore
and of course his line is out
but since the shape of time is namelessness
and time and matter are as Einstein says
intra-indicated
the question may be who will reel in who
not when
and it is clear for instance that nothing is
causal except in that one thing
follows another, evening and afternoon
are words.
              In the trees nearby a shower
of woodchips sprays up from the twinkling axe
and the sound of its bite strolls off to where
the Lord is
musing about plywood
and the loneliness brought to pass
so beyond all healing possibility
if I pray He listens
and gives me a soft little sock on the arm and arranges
as a gesture those
beautiful entanglings of shadow
the moon makes climbing through bare alder boughs
just the way Saint Bernard saw and praised it
as he lay down in his cold stream to unwrap the gift
of Faith with what he called Reason

though it may have been only what he wanted
and not what he knew that brought him strength
and sleep.
                    Oh teach me to glimmer
the wise man prays
or teach me to stay like the fisherman
alone
            all night waiting for the sea
that has no mother
that rocks and keens in mourning for its own
spacious music that gives then
takes away.

The Getaway

—for Lew (1944–1981)

I stop by to pick you up
     from death
and we accelerate just fast enough

to clear the mob of outraged mourners
     sprinting, bellowing
through their teeth about the coins

we've stolen from your eyes. Of course
     we're laughing,
lighting cigarettes and leaning

into the lovely weather of escape. Maybe
     both of us
have crossed the line and this is how

death starts, with some maniac fracture
     of the rules
of still decay and suffering, outlined

in the contract we shred and toss back
     into all the wind a flat
fucking fast convertible provides. We don't

know what this freedom means and don't care
     what we signed.
We've got the money and the voice

of Nat King Cole and this immense springtime,
     a backseat full of beer,
and daylight sweet and brighter than tears

and we're just *gone* down the two lane county roads
     where meadowlarks announce us,
where what we wish for has no waking

and no future and no price, and loss
     itself is lost and broke
and hitching sadly back to town.

Keats

When Keats, at last beyond the curtain
of love's distraction, lay dying in his room
on the Piazza di Spagna, the melody of the Bernini
Fountain "filling him like flowers,"
he held his breath like a coin, looked out
into the moonlight and thought he saw snow.
He did not suppose it was fever or the body's
weakness turning the mind. He thought, "England!"
and there he was, secretly, for the rest
of his improvidently short life: up to his neck
in sleigh bells and the impossibly English cries
of street vendors, perfect
and affectionate as his soul.
For days the snow and statuary sang him so far
beyond regret that if now you walk rancorless
and alone there, in the piazza, the white shadow
of his last words to Severn, "Don't be frightened,"
may enter you.

Event

The lovely women become ordinary.
Souls of the saints return to their rooms
in a compound bordered by brown grass.
The sun flames toward a blank black terminus

we think of as a door.
Hope itself is all that can be hoped for.

Even those angels singing about the Christ
shining new and bloody in a barn
in Bethlehem
saw that God had simply brought more hope

into the world
to keep it going. Wars, tortures, the curled

residue of mass executions fill the opposite
exertion, while the snowy moonlit hills
and foxfire meditations of beautiful old men
are wedged in the middle like extra spoons,

like the shape of the upper room
where Jesus said goodbye to his friends.

Like Rain Descending

Out of blackness rain dives down
like diamonds
into the new grass, into "the beautiful
uncut hair of graves," as Whitman called it.
Across eternity's light-drenched miles I imagine
my father, after long hours in the garden,
beckoning the angels by sighing
in his happy weariness. I think
folds of shadow under the rhododendron
are suffused with mystifications
so delicate the blossoms nearly speak,
though they know this would be wrong.
I think of serious and painful solace,
my sinews and bones strumming
a little tune when they open and admit
the fast falling dark cheekbone
of an ending. I think of numbers
set free in a huge bowl and Fabergé
weeping on the last train out
of St. Petersburg. I think of chastity
and kissing and the smile
of a Portuguese dwarf who once sold me
a watch when I needed the exact
betrayal, blades blinking in the leaves
and vice versa. Something with wings
departs and someone says, "Don't touch

the broken spots," but I do and my father
is like rain descending into the clarity
of darkness thinking of light, thinking
of what must be love's long embrace
and everything and no one enduring it.

The New Orpheus
—for Emma

As though windows had been nailed shut
I look out at the blank insides
of my eyes. Who lives here
in fire so deep it loves the water?
A handful of shells and a peacock moon
lie down in the dark of my arm.
Pins and needles, sorrow and salt: I'm trying
hard to match things up
with their Platonic other shinings.
I need more time for this
place I need to open like a door of rain,
like everything coming down
because of blue saturations of the unforgettable
and too hard to know. I'm giving myself just one
more lifetime of prying and pulling
at my hinges, beating the old empty roses
my daughter walks in, thinking I've been away
too long now, it's getting late, they're slamming
the other world and dousing the lights.
Rain and rain again, old winter. It's really dark
where she is. All night I lie awake, building a ladder
of light.

A Little Blues

There is no pain. A cracked
teacup rose says hover
in this fracture, your lips
like bees that love

the too ripe pear
nearby. Mist's in the air. Jerry
is filling his pipe again.
There's that song.

ACKNOWLEDGMENTS

Part title credits: p. 1: Robert Francis, "With the Year's Cooling," *Orb Weaver* (Wesleyan University Press, 1960); p. 29: John Ashbery, "The System," *Selected Poems* (Viking/Penguin, 1994); p. 61: D. Nurkse, "The Migraine," *The Fall* (Alfred Knopf, 2002).

Some of the poems in this volume originally appeared in periodicals and anthologies as follows:

American Literary Review: "A Christmas Ode After the Fashion of Michael Heffernan and Dedicated to Him and His Bride"
Ascent: "Trusting the Beads"
Cimarron Review: "Family Values"
Clackamas Literary Review: "The Montavilla Reveries," "Storm," "The Thirteenth Interval"
Colorado Review: "Why the River Is Always Laughing"
Connecticut Review: "Heaven," "1974"
Crazyhorse: "The New Orpheus"
Denver Quarterly: "Metamorphosis"
Field: "Backyard Astronomy"
Fine Madness: "Running"
Flint Hills Review: "To Build a Fire"
Gettysburg Review: "Apacatastasis," "History," "Event," "Zeno," "Bird Man Stranded," "Arrivals," "King's Ex"
Greensboro Review: "Sometimes at the Braille Calliope"
Hubbub: "The Counterchime," "If He Remembers June Light in Oslo," "The Double Suicide of Marriage," "Cole Porter"
Mid-American Review: "Galileo"
New Orleans Review: "He Writes to the Soul"
Northwest Review: "Confession," "Like Rain Descending"
Passages North: "Letter"
Poetry Northwest: "If the World Were Glass," "Story Time," "A Party on the Way to Rome"
Sou'wester: "All Day at the Brainard Pioneer Cemetery," "Keats"

Talking River Review: "The Eye Becomes Birds Because of War,"
    "A Little Blues"
Third Coast: "Unexpectation"
Turnrow: "Teleology of the Airhose," "Today"
Volt: "The Angels of Rescue"
Willow Springs: "The Getaway"
"History" was reprinted in *Harper's*, January 1997.
"A Party On the Way to Rome" appeared in *The Pushcart Prize: Best
    of the Small Presses XXIV*, ed. Bill Henderson (Wainscott, NY:
    Pushcart Press), 1999.
"He Writes to the Soul,'" appeared in *The Pushcart Prize: Best of the
    Small Presses XXVII*, ed. Bill Henderson (Wainscott, NY: Pushcart
    Press), 2003.
"The Toad Prince" appeared in *Deep Down Things*, ed. Schneider &
    McFarland (Pullman: Washington State Univ. Press), 1992.
"Why the River Is Always Laughing," and "We Who Have Found
    Wisdom" appeared in *Crossing the River: Poets of the Western
    United States*, ed. Ray Gonzales (Sag Harbor, NY: The Permanent
    Press), 1987.
"King of the Butterflies" appeared in *Sea of Voices, Isle of Story*,
    ed. Blue & Mergens (Eugene, OR.: Triple Tree Publishing), 2003,
    and was published also as a pamphlet chapbook titled *King of the
    Butterflies* (Omaha, NE.: Brady Press), 2003.
"Running" appeared in *March Hares*, ed. Bentley et al. (Seattle, WA:
    Fine Madness), 2003.
"Like Rain Descending," translated by Justin Hart, was published
    in *L'nea Imaginaria* (Quito, Ecuador), Spring 2002.
"The Counterchime," was honored with the Adrienne Lee Award,
    Hubbub magazine, 1996

I wish to thank the National Endowment for the Arts and the
Eastern Washington University Research and Creativity Committee for
fellowships that allowed me to complete the poems in this volume.
Thanks also to Joseph Millar, Dorianne Laux, Linda Bierds, Henry
Carlile, Nance Van Winckel, and David Luckert for their generous and
intelligent commentary.

ABOUT THE POET

CHRISTOPHER HOWELL is the author of eight collections of poems, including *Memory and Heaven* (1997) and *Just Waking* (2003). He has received the Washington State Governor's Award, two National Endowment for the Arts fellowships, a fellowship from the Artist Trust, and the Vachel Lindsay and Helen Bullis prizes. His work has made three appearances in the annual *Pushcart Prize* publication, most recently in 2002, and may be found also in many journals and anthologies. Since 1975 he has been director and principal editor for Lynx House Press and is now also senior editor at Eastern Washington University Press. He is on the Master of Fine Arts faculty of the Inland Northwest Center for Writers. Howell lives in Spokane with his wife, Barbara, and son, Evan. *Photo by W. T. Pfefferle.*

A NOTE ON THE TYPE

William Addison Dwiggins (1880–1956), an American designer and typographer, designed typefaces for the Linotype machine. In the 1930s and 1940s, he created the typographic house style at Alfred A. Knopf, New York.

These poems are set 10.6 pt. Electra with 16 pt. leading. Poem titles are set 18 pt. Electra Bold Cursive. The typesetting was done by Suzanne Harris at Integrated Composition Systems in Spokane, Washington.